MY JOU1

CW00327920

TEN YEAI_ _..

Copyright ©
Jennifer Buckle MBE 2005

Produced for Jennifer Buckle by
ORCHARD PUBLICATIONS
2 Orchard Close, Chudleigh, Devon TQ13 0LR
Telephone: (01626) 852714

I would like to dedicate this book to my wonderful family - Norman, Elizabeth, John and Jeremy.

ISBN 1898964 65 3

Printed by
Hedgerow Print, Crediton, Devon EX17 1ES

CONTENTS

My journey – ten years on   3

My accident in 1994   5

The work of the Devon Air Ambulance   7

Why do we need an air ambulance?   9

The garden   12

Welcome gardens   14

The challenge of thalidomide   17

Elizabeth   19

Oxford   21

John and Katherine   25

Norman and his art   28

The change in our orchard   31

The joy of honeybees   33

The letter from Number 10   36

A visit to Highgrove   39

Death by Gardening   41

The Quiet Garden Trust   44

Outreach to prison   47

Stumpwork mirror   49

The launch of the new air ambulance   52

And so to the future   54

MY JOURNEY – TEN YEARS ON

The first weekend of August brings many memories, because in 1994 on the first Saturday morning in August, I was airlifted to Derriford Hospital in Plymouth. The Devon Air Ambulance had been in mission barely two years and only flew on five days a week – in fact we were unaware that we even had such a service in the County. I think we knew that Cornwall had an air ambulance and later we found out that this was the first one, and ours in Devon was started five years later. We were thankful that one of the five days they flew was a Saturday, which was the day of the week that I severed my arm on the glass wall of our greenhouse.

Some two months later, Norman and I went to Exeter airport to meet the crew and to thank them for their work. We were surprised and really shocked to discover that this important service was completely funded by the efforts of people in the County of Devon. Recently I had retired from teaching so felt that I had the time to offer help to the Devon Air Ambulance Trust. During the next year I wrote a diary of how my injuries and treatment were progressing which I completed and called the book *A New Journey*. I dedicated it to Rob Mackie, Dave Hartland and Chris Wyatt, the crew on the air ambulance on the day I was taken to hospital, adding 'without them there would be no story'. This book has been enjoyed by many people, often helping those who are suffering pain or trying to adapt to disability. Also it has raised many thousands of pounds for the Devon Air Ambulance Trust.

Ten years on, in 2004 I was invited to visit Exeter Airport on the first weekend of August because the new EC135 helicopter would be arriving. In the morning the press were there and they gave good coverage of the event on the television and in the local papers. Some of the volunteers were there in the afternoon and I certainly had mixed feelings about saying farewell to the Bolkow, which had served the people of Devon so well. In fact we had used three helicopters during the twelve years of service, so this was not the one I had been airlifted in. As I drove towards Exeter, I realised that this day ten years ago I would have been on the stretcher in the helicopter, on my way to Accident and Emergency in Plymouth. It felt quite spooky that this was the same day that the new helicopter was arriving!

I mentioned this to Lyn Paver who is the General Manager and she said perhaps they could give me a flight. So, Steve Ford the pilot helped me on to the seat behind him, fixed the seatbelt and with Sarah, Jenny and Shirley we were off. We circled Exeter and then flew down the river Exe with wonderful views.

3

Steve and Rob Mackie had just returned from their conversion course in Glasgow and in Essex to learn to fly the new aircraft. It would start to be used in Devon in a few weeks time. I drove home to Woodland, near Ashburton that afternoon feeling very elated and privileged to know so many good people working for this Devon charity. Now ten years on, it seemed the time to reflect on everything that had happened to us as a family.

The fateful greenhouse where I spend many happy hours growing seeds and cuttings.

MY ACCIDENT IN 1994

"We are healed from suffering only by experiencing it to the full".

In August 1994 my life changed and it was not as I had planned for my retirement. I had to be airlifted to hospital in Plymouth for microsurgery to save my left arm. Accidents can happen so quickly and in unexpected ways, especially in the home and garden. Our wonderful garden gives Norman and me great pleasure, along with the hard work that goes with it. Pulling up weeds at ground level in the greenhouse, a long piece of ivy snapped and I fell off balance down through the glass wall. I was fortunate that I was able to get up and ran to the house for help. Perhaps it was because I sat on one of Elizabeth's large prickly pear cacti!

It was very obvious that I had damaged my left arm very badly and it was bleeding profusely. Norman fetched a pile of bath towels to wrap around it and then he ran to telephone 999 for an ambulance. It was driven along our country lanes, through Newton Abbot and along the main road to Torquay, with the ambulance siren blaring so I guessed it was urgent. The Devon Air Ambulance goes on line at 10.00 am in the summer but I had fallen through the greenhouse soon after 8.00 am. An urgent 999 call had gone to Exeter Airport where the air ambulance is based and they flew to Torbay Hospital to pick me up.

Later in the day I had a very long operation to save my arm and I was to discover that I had severed the ulna nerve, the main artery and most of the tendons in the lower part of the arm. I was given excellent care in the large Plastic Surgery and burns unit at Derriford Hospital. I began to realise how much my life had changed in that one moment in the greenhouse.

The following weeks and months meant daily and then continuous visits to the hospital for physiotherapy. Often the pain was unbearable but treatment at the pain clinic and by acupuncture helped. I started to write *A New Journey* as the function of my hand and arm began to improve. I kept a diary of the progress of what I could do again such as playing the piano, driving the car and everyday tasks. It surprised me how much we need to use both our hands for most activities, such as doing up shoelaces, using a knife and fork and I found that doing up a button was extremely difficult and painful.

That book was truly my faith story because I never doubted how much the Lord helped us through this difficult journey of our lives. How grateful we were for our family and our friends who supported us in so many ways.

5

We live in a wonderful area of South Devon, with views down a peaceful valley and to the hills beyond. We enjoy the changes of the seasons, especially the fresh colours of the leaves in spring. The first spring flowers are the snowdrops and primroses and they grow along the edges of fields and hedgerows. Then crocus and daffodils flower in the garden and we see the first sign of large queen bumblebees searching for pollen to feed their young underground. Then the bright yellow of the cowslips in the orchard which we grew at first from seeds and now they have naturalised. A bank of wild bluebells appear under the old apple trees. After my accident all this appeared more colourful and wonderful than ever before – in a way my second chance gave me a sensitive awareness of the beauty of our world and I learnt to be much more grateful for everything.

THE WORK OF THE DEVON AIR AMBULANCE

'Real people saving real lives'.

Several weeks after I had been airlifted we met the crew at Exeter airport. We wanted to thank them for saving me and it was during this visit we discovered that the service is paid for by the people of Devon. We felt we would like to help in any way we could and during the past ten years, our voluntary work for the Devon Air Ambulance Trust has become a part of our lives.

Piers le Cheminant is the Education Officer and he gives talks to schools across the county and if they have raised a large sum of money, he will arrange a drop-in by the helicopter. I have been to some of these occasions and of course it may not always be successful – I remember one secondary school in Plymouth had to wait for the third organised visit before the helicopter came. Probably the staff and pupils appreciated it all the more because they were very excited. Of course everyone knows that the service is there to help people and there is a chance that they will be disappointed if it is called out on a mission.

Piers and I have organised Helimed clubs for children, either for them as individuals or where they are interested in becoming involved through their groups such as Brownies and Cub Scouts. In one case, a whole country school joined with thirty-five pupils, after their headteacher had been rescued by the air ambulance. We organise a visit for the members to go to the airport for them to meet the crew and we make it quite a party with drinks and biscuits. There has to be a fruit cake for the crew and on occasions even a Devon cream tea with homemade jam. The Helimed members have their own magazine several times a year, a birthday card for the individual children and regular contact about what is going on. There was a big party at Crealy Park near Exeter for the fifth birthday of the helicopter service – I have never cut so many pieces of iced cake before!

When I was airlifted in 1994, the air ambulance only flew on five days each week and we were to discover that this was due to a lack of enough funds. It was not available on Tuesdays and Wednesdays but when the service was extended four years later, its use on these days was just as vital. It flies for eight hours each day, which was nearly a disaster for me because I fell through the greenhouse just after eight o'clock in the morning. I was taken to Torbay hospital by land ambulance, waiting for the air ambulance to become available two hours later.

Jennie Bond, the TV correspondent gave an amazing £261,000 to the Trust early in 2004 after taking part in *I'm a Celebrity...Get Me Out of Here!* It was decided to use some of the money immediately to extend the flying time by two hours each day, also an amazing piece of equipment was bought to help with navigation which would be fitted to the new helicopter which had been talked about and planned for. This is a GPS-linked moving map system to assist and increase the speed to an accident. It is well known that the first hour is vital in getting help and treatment to the patient. To be able to fly quickly to the Accident and Emergency department of a hospital will surely save lives and help with the healing of the patient.

The Devon Air Ambulance Trust is a charity and runs its own lottery, which has become a very important part of the income. It offers excellent prizes to the winners and the advert says 'Join our lottery now, Real people, Real lives making a Real difference'. People in Devonshire are very generous, especially as the years go by and there are wonderful stories to tell by patients whose lives have been changed by the air ambulance. Fund raising can be great fun and it ranges from charity dinners, fun runs, coffee mornings and quiz nights. I went to the big South West sheepdog trials on a very wet Saturday to receive a cheque for £2,000 and the Children's Hospice also received a cheque for the same amount. It was a wonderful example of generous sponsorship. I had just started to thank everyone on the microphone when the red helicopter flew over at the top of the hill. It was some poor person on their way to hospital but it was perfect timing for us.

A visit to Exeter Airport by one of the Junior Helimed groups.

WHY DO WE NEED AN AIR AMBULANCE?

Why do the people of Devon need an air ambulance? We live in a large county with very varied terrain from the tors on Dartmoor to coastal footpaths and with over nine thousand miles of roads. Many of these are unclassified and can be meandering, remote and hilly. All the routes across the county are affected by the vast influx of tourists during the summer and it is noticeable how many more vehicles are on the roads in the last ten years.

Road traffic accidents account for more than 30% of the work of the helicopter and other missions are to rescue walkers, equestrians and of course people who have accidents in the home, the garden and the workplace. Since the service started in 1992 it has been possible for emergency medical assistance to reach any isolated part of Devon within nineteen minutes of a 999 call being received by the crew at Exeter airport.

The service not only takes lifesaving missions but it can also reduce patient deterioration by getting them to hospital quickly. The first air ambulance service to start was in Cornwall in 1987 and over the years many other counties have started the operation – across to Kent and Essex and up to the Midlands. No financial support is available from local or national government and because the Ambulance Service NHS Trust controls the use of the helicopter (and supplies the paramedics and medical equipment) no funding is available from the National Lottery. The services in London and Scotland, however, are funded by the NHS.

Fund raising has been a great effort and on July 7th 1998 there was the launch of seven day flying but the Trust needed to raise £1.2 million that year to pay for the extended service. Over the ten years, my role as a volunteer has grown from working with children as junior members to emptying collecting tins in local pubs and shops, which gives me the opportunity to explain to more people about the service. Also I may go to a function to receive a cheque and to give a vote of thanks or a brief talk. There are many groups that need a speaker and it may be the WI, a Probus Club, the Inner Wheel, or gardening clubs and many others. I have a wide selection of colour slides that give an illustrated input of what goes on across the county. My book *A New Journey* was published by Orchard Publications and launched in February 1999. In the last five years I have sold over 2,000 copies of the book.

In May 1999 I was invited to Exeter Airport when Princess Anne visited to give the Royal seal of approval. This was the first time that a member of the Royal family had visited any of the air ambulance services. It was a wet and

9

At the launch of my book (A New Journey) with Chris Wyatt, paramedic.

Dominic (paramedic), Steve (pilot), Graham (Director of DAAT), the author, Nev (engineer), A. Brunton (Orchard Publications), Gary and Chris (paramedics).

misty morning and we were escorted across the runways from the main terminal. We were told that the Princess Royal's helicopter would be late because of the poor weather, so we waited inside a large hangar feeling very wet and cold. When she arrived she was wearing a lovely bright red suit and she spent a long time talking to the crew and looking inside the helicopter. Paramedics took out one of the stretchers to show her what it was like. Then she met Ann Thomas who began the idea of having an air ambulance in Devon after the family lost their young son in a road traffic accident. Princess Anne moved across to talk to some of us who had been patients. Jeanette had been thrown from her horse and badly injured and I guess this interested the keen royal rider. Then she came to me and asked why I had been airlifted. I explained that I had had an accident falling through the wall in our greenhouse – "and why didn't you use the door?" she asked, so I told her our joke "never trust ivy in the greenhouse". I was pulling up weeds along the path and a long piece of ivy snapped, throwing me off balance through the glass. Sarah, who had had a horrific car accident talked to her next and she was very concerned to hear how we are all getting on. Then volunteers, staff and many others were introduced to her.

I had asked if I could give Princess Anne a copy of *A New Journey*, so it had to be inspected by the police and palace staff before I could present it to her. I often wonder if she has read it or passed it to her mother to read! We all had an extremely exciting day and it was a superb way to recognise everyone who is involved with this charity.

Princess Anne chats to Sarah, the author and Jeanette - with Ann Thomas, who began the fund raising for a Devon Air Ambulance, in the foreground.

THE GARDEN

Our England is a garden
And such gardens are not made
By singing "oh, how beautiful"
And sitting in the shade.

Norman and I were married in 1957 and we lived in a small semi-detached house in Enfield, Middlesex with a sloping front garden and a larger piece at the back. We enjoyed growing plants for colour and we had a small piece for a vegetable patch. Norman had always been a gardener because his parents had a large and productive garden in his Buckinghamshire home when he was growing up. He remembers visiting his grandfather's allotment, this being the highlight of their visit to grandpa. It was beside the mainline railway and the canal, so it was also a good place to see the steam trains. When his father was in the Navy during the Second World War, Norman helped his mother with the digging and the growing of vegetables and soft fruit. Through this he developed an empathy with the garden by watching the growth of the crops.

My memories of gardens were not quite so happy! I lived with my parents in Winchmore Hill in north London and at each house we had a garden. My mother loved to have flowers such as asters to pick for the house – my father always had a frown on his face when the lawn needed cutting or the edges trimmed. The small vegetable patch had to have Brussels sprouts but somehow they were never successful as my mother declared; "they are not much larger than peas". It never seemed to be much of an enjoyable pastime – my mother preferred to play tennis and my father enjoyed his cricket and golf.

Norman has certainly encouraged me to be a gardener and now that we live in Woodland, we have a beautiful country garden, which includes an orchard with a small stream flowing through it. There are cider apple trees, new and old dessert and cooking apples, plum, black cherry and soft fruit bushes in the garden. The orchard was just the right place to keep hives of honeybees and certainly our crops have improved with these insects contributing to the pollination work.

'A Garden of Fragrant Flowers will be a garden of bees and butterflies'. Our Woodland garden had a large well-stocked herbaceous border when we moved in and we have added buddleia and a bed of michaelmas daisies, which give food for all insects at the end of the summer. A silver *Pittisporum* tree, a present for our silver wedding anniversary will really hum with hundreds of bees for about ten days in July, when the tiny dark mauve flowers are open. They must be full of nectar, much needed to stock up the combs in the beehives.

The vegetable garden is a great joy and we try a new crop most years, and recently we have enjoyed sweet corn and pink fir apple potatoes. We always grow runner beans and marrows (the latter grown on last year's compost heap), spinach, leeks and a great variety of salads. The seeds are sown early in the spring in the greenhouse, potted on and then planted out when the soil has warmed up. Years ago the kitchen garden would have grown a far wider variety of produce, including herbs for the use in the kitchen and these would have included flowers such as lavender, poppies and mallow. We often grow rows of clarkia, which remind me of our garden in London, larkspur and marigolds in between the rows of vegetables. Many of the old ideas of gardening seem to be returning especially in National Trust properties and it is exciting to see.

In 1998 we made a living willow hedge as shade or as a windshield for the main vegetable bed. It has been a great success, and we have been able to supply many other peoples' gardens with the prolific annual growth that is cut off each autumn.

Ten years ago our garden pond was started, just before my accident so the two upper levels with a waterfall had to wait to be completed a few years later. The pond was made on a slope above the lawn that never seemed to have a purpose. Somehow the sound of water in a garden alters the dimensions of the place. It is very peaceful and soothing, and creatures such as newts, frogs or toads, water beetles live there – and later in the summer months, the beauty of caddis and dragonflies can be seen.

The garden was featured on Westcountry Television in 1996 and several children from a local primary school took part – of course, the honeybees were an important part of the programme. As the years have gone by many people (in fact, hundreds) have visited, inspected and enjoyed our garden and we have raised over £10,000 for the Devon Air Ambulance Trust. Our cream teas are known as 'the best in the west'.

WELCOME GARDENS

We became part of the Devon Air Ambulance Welcome Garden Scheme. Claire from the Devon Air Ambulance Trust visited us one wet, dreary January morning and we tramped around the garden and orchard in our wellies. She said that it would be suitable and we agreed to open one midsummer weekend in June. Since then we have opened our garden regularly and it has become part of our lives, giving an added purpose to our gardening programme.

The first year we provided light lunches and teas, and our dear friend Yvette came to stay so that she could mastermind the kitchen arrangements. We needed plenty of volunteers to take the orders and others to carry the trays to and fro the garden – and we were lucky with a sunny weekend. Since then we have had wet days, including one Sunday when cream teas were served throughout our cottage, in every available space. It was amazing how the helpers managed! We always have a plant stall, Devon Air Ambulance Trust teddies for sale because Ambrose Airbear is the mascot for the helicopter, and honey and wax candles. We have raised a huge total, at the same time as giving enjoyment to many people. It is surprising how visitors enjoy the vegetable garden, perhaps because fewer people grow them these days.

On the Saturday that I was airlifted to Derriford from Torbay hospital in 1994 Captain Rob Mackie was the pilot that day and I said that he really ought to visit our garden. The first time we opened the garden, during the afternoon we heard the familiar helicopter noise and the small red helicopter appeared over the trees, circling around above us. I was so exited and everyone ran out to wave as it landed in the field next door. What a treat – everyone ran down the road and over the fields to look inside the helicopter. Rob said that he had never known me to be speechless before! Of course, the crew were served a cream tea and their photograph was taken standing by the front white gate, which was used as the cover picture for *A New Journey*.

Two years later the helicopter visited again and that weekend friends from the Beekeeping Club were around the garden to talk to people. Stuart and Nigel were the two paramedics on board this time, and as Nigel is a beekeeper too, he must have felt at home as Glyn told everyone about the life of bees. He had brought a small swarm, only about a teacupful in size, which amused us all. Then the telephone rang and the helicopter had to leave in a hurry to go to an accident in Dartmouth – they were halfway there from our garden, thank goodness.

The Welcome Garden scheme has obviously added to the funds, as well as giving opportunities for the public to find out more about the work of the service. We have enjoyed visiting other gardens too.

Summertime in the orchard.

A quiet place to sit, to read or to paint.

15

The orchard is a wonderful place to run and climb the trees, and here the Blanchard family and some of their grandchildren have enjoyed a barbecue.

One of the many groups of visitors.Can you see a swarm of bees on one of the apple trees?

THE CHALLENGE OF THALIDOMIDE

In the late 1950s tranquillisers became very popular and it seemed to be the safe and helpful way to achieve calm in an increasingly hectic world. In over forty countries, mothers took a tranquillising pill that was said to be non-toxic and with no side effects and even safe for pregnant women. That wonder pill was thalidomide and eight thousand babies were horribly poisoned by it, entering the world with terrible deformities.

Everywhere there was horror and shame when the births made the newspaper headlines in 1961. The drug had been made in Germany and it had been sold on all over the world under the premise that it was safe. After it was withdrawn, some women knew they had been given thalidomide and they had to wait for the birth of their baby to know if there was any damage. Over four hundred babies survived in this country and of course, Elizabeth is one of them.

I had been sent by my family doctor to a local hospital in north London during the early weeks of pregnancy because I had terrible sickness. I remember the sister on the ward touching me on my arm, saying; "never mind mother, we have a wonderful new drug which will help you". I would not know that it was thalidomide or 'Distaval' to give it its other name, until Elizabeth was two years old. By then we were living in Devon because during the week that she was born, Norman was offered a job in Torquay. We thought that a new start in Devon would be good for us after the shock of the birth. We were obviously concerned that our daughter would have difficulties with her short arms and missing thumbs and felt that we should try to give her the best living conditions that we could.

Ten years after the first babies were born in Britain the legal battle for compensation was in deadlock. The drug had been prescribed on the National

A school photograph of John and Elizabeth, aged five and nine years.

17

Health but the government denied all responsibility and it was up to the families to pursue their own efforts for recognition and compensation. The Lady Hoare Fund for Thalidomide Children was set up when Mary Hoare persuaded her husband, then Lord Mayor of London, to make it his charity. She went to see a large group of babies in 1962 who were living at Chailey Heritage in Sussex. This was a special home for severely disabled children. Lady Hoare was overwhelmed by the babies she saw and she wanted to help the families. She was a lovely lady and often came to Devon especially when the children were having a pony-trekking holiday at Hexworthy, on Dartmoor. Elizabeth enjoyed several holidays there with Judy and Rob Shephard who ran adventure holidays. Later she also went canoeing on the River Dart and across the Great Lakes of the United States of America.

This was a challenge for us as parents, especially with our concerns about her schooling and we approached three primary schools before Elizabeth was accepted. I think these situations are easier nowadays because the integration of disabled people into society is much more acceptable. We were extremely lucky that we met helpful people along the way and Elizabeth has been very purposeful in her life. She has known what she has wanted to do – 'to help to save the environment' and she has certainly followed that mission. We are very proud of her and also of John in the way that they both work hard and tackle the challenges in their lives.

John and Elizabeth (and 'Rusty').

ELIZABETH

Look deep into nature and then you will understand everything better.
Albert Einstein

Our daughter Elizabeth was born in 1960 and even as a tiny baby she loved the flowers in our London garden. Then, when she was a few months old we moved to Devon, partly to give her a larger area for her to play in as she grew. This she must have appreciated as she spent most of her time outside and she would bring worms to the back doorstep for us to see, as soon as she could move around. She was fascinated with living things, especially when we went to the seaside where she would collect shells and peer and dip into rock pools for hours. Elizabeth wanted to learn the names of every plant and animal and to understand how they lived, and she loved to look at books – we did not have television in those days.

Following her years at school, she chose Durham University to read botany. Much of the work was done in the laboratory, which gave her a scientific approach and taught her how living things are interdependent on each other. Elizabeth says "I had always turned over cow pats and I still do – a cow pat is a living world in itself, full of insects and fungi growing on them". Apparently cow pats have changed over the years, as cows are now dosed with strong chemicals and this has changed the life of a cow pat.

After her degree, it was obvious that Elizabeth would look for work concerned with the natural environment. For a while she worked voluntarily for the Devon Wildlife Trust, going on to work for the Dartmoor National Park to survey and map the vegetation on Dartmoor. During this time she lived at home with us, and her Ford Escort car was always full of folders, maps, muddy boots and wet clothes. Then she moved to a post with Nature Conservation in the Yorkshire Dales where for three years she continued the vegetation mapping and working with farmers and landowners over the designation of special areas.

In 1988, Scotland had a recruitment drive for staff and she was given a job in Argyll on the West Coast. Elizabeth was dealing with nature in its raw wildness often in terrible weather. She went out in small boats to count seals and she was thrilled that there were still new discoveries to be made. A few years later she applied for promotion and she went to Lanark, in central Scotland. She was dealing with the wide view of all the issues that affect the land with the often conflicting interests of the people who lived there. By 2001, Elizabeth felt she wanted to concentrate on a particular project so she applied for a post with English Nature to work with local communities in County Durham. Industries had kept the local communities strong for hundreds of years but with the closure of these, people needed to find alternative ways of living off the land and its natural resources. Elizabeth's project aimed to help these people to clarify and establish what they wanted for their local communities. Then she applied to the Heritage Lottery Fund who eventually promised millions of pounds for a five-year project, that will enable these people to do wonderful things for their local environment.

With my daughter Elizabeth at her Graduation ceremony at Durham University. This was after the Graduation in the Castle on the green near the Cathedral.

OXFORD

In 2003, Elizabeth and Jeremy moved to Oxford. She had met Jeremy during her work in Scotland when he asked Scottish Natural Heritage for advice about his woodlands and plum orchards. In fact we first met him when he came to John and Katherine's wedding in Colchester. After her work in County Durham, English Nature asked Elizabeth to take on a project based in Oxford, to help people in different European countries to consider the long-term effects of climate change.

This would be the first time that a group of people concerned with the environment would work together to tackle the issues of the impact of climate change on natural systems. This is an issue of global concern and it needs countries' money and commitment to work together. There is much talk in the media at the moment but not enough action.

Elizabeth helped this project's success in getting a large amount of European funds and it has now started as a three year project in Northern European countries to try to show what will happen as sea levels rise and climatic conditions change. Will our natural systems and wildlife be able to adapt to these new conditions? As a beekeeper, I can already see the results of temperature changes on my colonies of honeybees and how the weather affects the plants and trees they need to forage.

Elizabeth's deep interest and concern for the environment started when she was very young and so her training, experience and commitment continues.

It was a new experience for her to live in a city like Oxford. Elizabeth and Jeremy found a flat near the centre from where she was able to walk to work at the University's Environmental Change Institute every day – anyway it is hopeless having a car in Oxford because of the congestion and parking problems, so most people cycle or walk if they can. We went to stay for a long weekend and the weather was wet and windy, so we not only walked but we were blown everywhere! It was a wonderful few days visiting the Bodleian Library, the museums and many colleges with their fine chapels and carefully tended gardens.

What a delight in the chapel of Keble College to find the *Light of the World* with its glorious colours and detail. Holman Hunt painted the picture in 1853 and it was hung in the Royal Academy the following year. He began to paint when he was twenty one but he did not complete it for eight years because he wanted to perfect the dawn, which he found in Bethlehem. It is from Revelation Chapter 3: 'Behold I stand at the door and knock. If any man hear my voice and open the door, I will come into him and will sup with him and he with me'. The painting is full of allegorical symbols but Elizabeth had heard of one that was not described on the information leaflet. When a tourist party had left the chapel, we went to have a closer look. Sure enough, half hidden in the foliage above the door we could see a bat of no recognisable species.

First we bought some postcards of the painting and then a very large poster, which we have framed in gold and it hangs in our dining room. It is a reminder of my childhood days because there was a picture of it at home and also it helps us to remember our recent stay in Oxford.

Oxford is part of my childhood because at the start of the war in 1939 I was evacuated to Headington near Oxford to stay with Great Aunt Lizzie. She had run a most respected Dame School for many years and she was quite old when I met her, and rather scary. Luckily in some ways, I did not need to stay for long as my parents decided that it would be better for me to come home to them in north London, because there had been no air raids for many weeks. Soon afterwards we had the London blitz and every night we spent sleeping in a brick shelter at the end of the garden.

Aunt Lizzie's School, in the 1920s.

22

St. Andrew's Church, early 1900s.

Headington is mentioned in the Domesday Book as 'Hedintone' and was called the royal village, with Henry I (died 1135) being the last English king to reside there. The parish church we now see was established from 1142 with its Norman Arch and part of the chancel dating from that time. Since then it has been added to, changed and restored.

Aunt Lizzie's school was known as a well respected private Dame School, a kind of kindergarten with about thirty children. My mother used to talk about some of the children in the photograph. She remembered the twins sitting in the front who were part of the Berry family, who had twelve children. They ran the bakery in the village and delivered with a horse-drawn cart. Wonderful family memories of long ago came back the day we visited Headington.

Lizzie was my maternal grandmother's youngest sister and I have postcards and photographs of the family home in Headington where they were all born. When we stayed with Elizabeth in Oxford recently, she took us to the village on the Sunday morning which happened to be Mothering Sunday. There was a service just finishing in the Parish Church so we went in to visit and we took photographs

23

St. Andrews' Church in 2004.

of the church and the family home along St. Andrews Lane. When we compared these with the old photographs taken a hundred years ago it was amazing to see how little it had changed. This was a special day for me because I felt the memories of so many years ago. I am sure that my mother, who had died just after my accident, was with us and rejoicing. She had really loved Oxford and would have been so pleased that Elizabeth was working there all these years later.

JOHN AND KATHERINE

John is three years younger than Elizabeth and when he was only two or three years old, he loved to build or make things. Of course he had 'lego' and 'meccano' but John had a gift to turn a cardboard box into a church, cathedral or a theatre. He had constructed a grand Westminster Abbey out of card from pictures in books but then we visited on a day trip to London on the train. When he got home all the inside was altered to be correct – the seats, the altar and even the colour of the carpets.

During his teenage years John joined the Newton Abbot Amateur Dramatics, helping to make scenery and taking part in the pantomimes or the musical *Half a Sixpence*. Eventually he wrote to the new Theatre Royal in Plymouth and worked as a props carpenter. This led to a permanent post involved with making 'props', and one of his first jobs was a new production of *Peter Pan*, with Bonnie Langford in the lead role.

John learnt the skills of the theatre work 'at the coal face' and he obviously loved the life that went with it. He has met many famous and interesting people and gained a high level of experience. Probably one of the most interesting and challenging pieces of work was refurbishing the set for *The Sound of Music*, not only for the stage of the Theatre Royal but to be able to be packed into a plane so that they could fly the whole show to Iceland! His postcards from there showed how much it was a good experience for him too.

John worked at Plymouth for five years helping to build many shows, which transferred to the West End or toured Britain and abroad. Then he set up a scenery building workshop and spent three years working as a production carpenter for Apolla Leisure. He toured with shows such as *Chess, South Pacific, 42nd Street* and *Barnum*. After that, he went to Worcester to be master carpenter and stage manager at the Swan Theatre before moving to Colchester to re-open the scenic workshop, and later becoming Production Manager.

At Colchester he met Katherine, who worked in the office at the theatre. We had heard a little about her because he told us that he had visited a friend in Brompton Hospital. She had cystic fibrosis and I knew about this disease because several young children I had taught early in my career, had died from it. Cystic fibrosis is Britain's most common life threatening disease, affecting over 7,500 young people. The average life expectancy for someone with it is about thirty years.

Katherine and John became engaged and planned their wedding to take place in August 1998. All the family and friends that attended knew it was a very special occasion. Katherine looked like a little princess and her parents Jane and Nick and her grandparents were so proud. Her sister Rebecca was one of the bridesmaids. The reception was held on the lawns of a hotel by an idyllic river and John and Katherine danced long into the evening.

Katherine was twenty one when she married John, so we all had hope that they would have many happy years together. Soon after their marriage, Katherine agreed to put her name on a heart and lung transplant list. Her health was very good for the first year and she was able to go to the theatre to work but then her health started to deteriorate. She was prone to have chest infections but she became resistant to the treatments and she needed oxygen a lot of the time. John bought another long-haired dachshund puppy to keep Katherine and 'Rusty',who was two years old, company and they were great fun together. Katherine loved coming to stay with us in Devon but the last time that they came, she was very unwell and needing oxygen most of the time.

John and Katherine's wedding

26

I have a book *Glimpses of the Divine* written by Bishop Cyril Bulley and it has readings and prayers for each day. On February 22nd 2000, part of the prayer 'Tend thy sick ones, O Lord Christ. Rest thy weary ones. Bless the dying ones. Soothe the suffering ones' was comforting because we knew that Katherine had been rushed to Brompton Hospital after being very ill for the past few months. A phone call from Jane the following morning told us that Katherine had died peacefully at 4.40 am.

Elizabeth drove down from Scotland to be with John and to help with the funeral arrangements. For Norman and me it was the worst situation we have faced or ever tried to cope with. Family and friends found it hard to know what to say but we know there were many prayers said for all of us. Eighteen months on we returned to the little church where John and Katherine had such a joyful wedding, but this time it was for her funeral. It was so good that Clive, their best man, travelled from Newton Abbot to be with us and Keith, Norman's brother was there too.

We went back to John's house to meet everyone and have

Elizabeth and Jeremy.

some refreshments – there were so many young people there wearing black. We felt we had had such a short time to get to know our daughter-in-law but we were glad that she had enjoyed coming to stay here with us in Devon. Not long before she died Katherine had told John that she badly wanted to be well enough to come again in the spring, but it was not to be.

Messages and cards were here when we returned home from Colchester and one of these was from the Dartmouth branch of the Mothers' Union, which is still beside Katherine's photograph; 'Some people come into our lives for a while and leave footprints on our hearts, and we are never the same'. That message just said it perfectly for us.

NORMAN AND HIS ART

*'Art is the unceasing effort to compete with the beauty of flowers and nature –
and never succeeding'.*
Marc Chagall.

Some years ago, Norman's art group first came to spend a day in our garden
and orchard drawing or painting – it is part of their summer programme. There
have been some wonderful results and in fact, two of the paintings hang in our
cottage. Of course, a cream tea is served about four o'clock when they are here,
and everyone can view each others work.

I met Norman in a north London Art Club in the 1950s once I had returned
home to live with my parents after finishing at teacher training college.   A
school friend Sylvia and I were invited by an art teacher to go with her to the club
in Southgate. Norman would wander in and peer over our easels and I can
remember he would make humorous comments every time! My mother was not
too keen when I first took him home because I had explained that he usually
worked in the 'Life' room. "He cannot be a very nice boy", she would say. We
soon realised that he was kind and thoughtful and he has been a wonderful husband
to me for forty seven years.

Norman regrets not being able to go to an art college when he was young
because he had always enjoyed drawing. Opportunities for further education
were more limited in those days, so the Southgate Club offered a good opportunity
to develop painting as a hobby.   After we were married and bringing up our
family, there were few chances to paint (other than windows and walls!). Now
during the last ten years Norman has used every opportunity to develop his skills
and has produced some excellent results.

When I first met Norman he painted in oils as he liked the textures he could
produce with them. Then watercolours became more popular, so he decided to
use them partly because they are more convenient to use when painting outside
the studio. He prefers to paint landscapes, especially Dartmoor where he captures
the grandeur of the moors, their vastness, mystery and rugged beauty. Boats and
harbours have always held a fascination for him and painting holidays in Cornwall,
Guernsey and Scotland have provided attractive subject matter.

Painting has opened up a new world for Norman, offering lasting friendships,
meeting other painters and professional artists on the holidays and at workshops.

28

It has led him to see and to appreciate so much more, whether it is a landscape or a still life subject. A sky is not just blue but a gradation of many colours – clouds are not just grey but by looking at them more closely, you can see the colours of a rainbow forming. It is important to analyse a view and to try to interpret the colours to use, as well as presenting the perspective and to do this with your own particular style.

A watercolour painting of Newton Abbot

He has returned primarily to oil painting using paints which can be mixed with water instead of oil and solvents like turpentine and white spirit. The paints are genuine oil colours made from modified linseed or safflower oil and work in just the same way as conventional oil colours but without the associated smells and disadvantages. Brushes, palette and any 'accidents' are simply cleaned with soap and water. Who now says that oil and water do not mix?

Painting in oils is not as convenient when working outdoors on a landscape. As oil takes longer to dry than watercolour it is more difficult to finish a view in one visit and, as weather conditions are seldom the same on consecutive days, the painting has to be finished at home. Having said that, the spontaneity of

Brent Tor, Dartmoor, in oils.

working quickly to get a painting finished in one visit greatly adds to the vitality which it may be difficult to achieve or maintain in the studio.

Norman often makes a sketch of the subject, usually an ink drawing with watercolour washes for colour reference, particularly of any colour which attracted him to the scene or subject in the first place. One sees and learns so much more of the subject as one draws and explores the picture before one. Photographs also help greatly for later reference. He really enjoys sketching and painting as a pastime and is happy whatever the subject, be it landscape, still life, portrait or life, trying to achieve a good representation. The result may not wholly please him every time but he is never more relaxed or absorbed than with a pen, pencil or brush in his hand.

In painting it is always advisable to step back from the picture you are working on to reflect on it - a good policy in all aspects of life.

He feels that painting as well as gardening, which is another satisfaction in his life, brings us closer to the wonder of creation and the magical beauty and peace of nature. Certainly the examples of his paintings on the walls in our cottage show his joy and talents. Everyone who comes to visit us enjoy his changing exhibits.

THE CHANGE IN OUR ORCHARD

Part of our Woodland garden is a small orchard with a stream running through it. There are old apple trees still bearing fruit alongside the ones we planted when we moved here. There are five hives of honeybees and a small shed where I keep all of the beekeeping equipment. There is a plaque on this that states 'a beekeeper lives here', but I have not had to resort to that yet! There is a good smell of honey and wax as you open the door as I keep spare boxes of honeycomb in there.

The grass in the orchard was always cut regularly during the summer after the farmers next door reduced their flock of sheep – these had been good at cropping our grass earlier on. One area that could not be cut easily is where the bank of cowslips grow. This was a great success starting from just a few plants grown from seed, but now they are happy to naturalise themselves. We had been unaware that cutting the grass so regularly was not helpful to the wildflowers.

Elizabeth advised us to cut a few paths through the orchard instead, leaving the rest of the meadow uncut until late summer so that the flowers have a chance to flower and set seed. This was based on her experience of the traditional management of hay meadows in the Yorkshire Dales, which are a glorious carpet of colour in the summer months.

So this is what we do each summer and over the years we have seen the wild flowers increase – their seeds must have remained dormant in the soil for many years. Each year different flowers seem to dominate – ox-eye daisies will be abundant one year and less the next, whereas vetches, marsh thistles and knapweed give a purple haze. Recently bird's foot trefoil and lady's bedstraw have flowered in large yellow patches that seem to have attracted greater numbers of small blue butterflies. One cannot fail to have faith when you look at their perfect tiny wings of a translucent blue sheen, flitting from flower to flower.

Visitors enjoy walking along the cut paths through the waving grass heads and are able to admire the complexity of flower colours, usually ending up perched on the prostrate boughs of a huge stooping apple tree. This tree may have fallen over a hundred years ago but continues to grow upwards from where its branches touch the ground. It is a picture of pink blossoms in April and later the russet apples form although nowadays very few reach maturity, perhaps because the tree is used so much for climbing. There are deep fissures and holes in its main trunk offering refuge for insects and probably mice. It is good to leave branches and stacks of dead wood about for this purpose of providing homes and food for wild creatures. We have put out a tube and a layered box full of tubes to provide a nesting environment for mason and leafcutter bees, although the latter species always come into the greenhouse in June carrying sections of green leaf. They disappear under several plant pots on the shelf to make their nesting tubes out of the leaves, in which they lay their eggs.

The countryside is changing all the time, with hedges and woodlands being grubbed up – consequently wild creatures are losing their natural habitat – so it is good to try to provide for them in as many ways that we can. Even in a small garden an area can be left for wildflowers and it is such a joy to watch all the insects at work. We have a large bed of michaelmas daisies in the main garden that provide food for butterflies and bees of every kind during the summer months. Then they need to store up food for the long winter months.

Visitors fron Exmouth enjoy the wild flowers.

THE JOY OF HONEYBEES

Marriage, birth or burying
News across the seas,
All your sad or marrying
You must tell the bees.

Telling the bees is an old custom and traditionally the head of the household would tell the bees of important events affecting the family, as it was believed that the bees would be insulted if they were not the first to be told of any good or bad news. Now I would never have believed this years ago but since becoming a beekeeper I do believe it is true. Soon after we brought bees to our orchard we were burgled and many valuable as well as small sentimental things were taken. I was angry and upset, and remember going down to the end of the garden close to the beehive to have a good cry. Within a day or two, the first hive was empty – the colony had gone. When I told someone in the beekeeping club they exclaimed: "You didn't tell them properly, so they took on your grief and left". Since then I have heard of other very similar stories.

I became interested in bees over twenty years ago when I was teaching in Barton, Torquay and the subject of bees came into the curriculum. I went to an evening class taken by Henry Luxton for a year and so began my joy of honeybees. The children in school were fascinated and Ron Brown visited us there and I

A swarm of honey bees under the bird table.

could see the potential for the children's learning. Henry and Ron are two of the most experienced bee-keepers in Devon. Ever since, it has been an important mission to share this with others, young and old. We kept a National hive of bees in the garden in Highweek School, in Newton Abbot, where I taught for many years and the children learned so much from observing the bees and helping with their care. They helped me to extract the honey and bottle it, and of course enjoyed eating the honey. The parents queued to buy a jar, especially if their child had an allergy – it is well known that honey will help if it comes from the local area.

So what is honey? It is made from nectar, a sweet liquid produced by flowering plants to attract insects for the purpose of pollinating the flowers. The worker bees carry the nectar back to the hive to be made into honey to provide a store of food for themselves and their young. Throughout history, honey has been used in many ways, from currency to culinary, from cold cures to hangover relief, as an energy booster or as a moisturiser. It is used on ulcers and wounds to assist healing and is one of the purest, most natural, healthy and versatile foods around.

I have used the 'Three Bs' as one of the Mothers' Union talks that I give – Belief, Bees and the Bible – these three 'B's' are genuinely important to me too. Honey is first mentioned in the bible in Genesis chapter 43, verse 11: 'carry down the man a present – a little balm, and a little honey, some spices and myrrh, nuts and almonds'. There are four references to bees in the bible and nearly sixty about honey.

Bees have been a source of ideas for embroidery for me, especially in the stumpwork mirror I worked, which included flowers, insects and the creatures seen in our garden. The mirror hangs in the hallway of our cottage. There are endless stories and rhymes about bees which make it attractive and easy for children to learn about them; 'It's all very well to steal the bees' honey, but ...... if you are stung it's not very funny', and 'bees.....every bee that ever was, is partly sting and partly buzz'.

When people talk about honey bees they always mention the fact that they sting and also that they swarm. Sometimes they will swarm in the summer months if the colony in the hive has built up, so that there is not enough room for them. The queen bee may lay as many as 1000-1500 eggs each day for the first few years but as she gets older and slows down the colony plan to make a successor. They build wax queen cells which are shaped like an egg and the larvae inside will be fed with royal jelly to develop into a queen bee. The old queen will then prepare to swarm to find a new home.

The swarm may settle in a bush or tree while scout bees fly off and search for a new site. The bees in the photogragh came to the bird table in our back garden. In the evening I collected them in a basket hive, called a skep, and put them into an empty hive in the orchard. Skeps were used to house bees over a hundred years ago until we made wooden hives for them. Beekeepers are pleased to collect swarms in the summer and a phone call to the local council offices should direct you to a local beekeeper.

'Beekeeping is a business that requires the greatest amount of attention to small details so the good beekeeper is generally more or less cranky'.

C. P. Dadent.

Collecting the swarm in a basket skep.

35

THE LETTER FROM NUMBER 10

In November 2001, a letter came addressed to me from the Prime Minister. I did not open it immediately because we took note of the message on the front of the envelope which stated 'parcel in beehive'. While we investigated the parcel, the white envelope was left sitting on the table. The spare white hive outside on the edge of the front path is a useful post box for large parcels. When I read the letter it informed me that my name was being submitted to the Queen, with a recommendation that her Majesty may be graciously pleased to approve that I be appointed a Member of the Order of the British Empire (MBE). It went on to say 'before doing so, the Prime Minister would be glad to know that this would be agreeable to you'.

I have heard how some people refuse but felt that this was an unexpected honour – but I could not discuss it with anyone except Norman – the letter warned that this information is 'in strict confidence!' So I completed the enclosed form saying 'yes' and returned this to Number 10 Downing Street. I would hear nothing more until the end of the year, and by that time we had almost forgotten about it.

That Christmas brought bad weather and neither John nor Elizabeth could get home. The day before New Years Eve the telephone rang and it was the Western Morning News to congratulate me – and then another local paper, the Herald Express also phoned to ask if someone could come to take photographs. So, it had really happened and I was to be awarded the MBE for 'Services to the Community of Devon'. Apparently this was for my early work with playgroups, toy libraries for handicapped children, bees and schools and more recent charity work for the Devon Air Ambulance Trust.

Now we could tell Elizabeth and John the news – Elizabeth mentioned that too many pop stars and footballers get honoured but I assured her I was not one of these! Once the New Years Honours list appeared in local papers, we received wonderful cards and letters, some from people we had not seen for many years and these we treasure along with all the photographs that were taken.

And so we were invited to Buckingham Palace on Wednesday 20th February 2002 for my investiture. I could take three guests to watch the ceremony and it would take place at 11.00am. We sent John the parking ticket for the Palace and we travelled to London the day before, meeting Elizabeth at the hotel where we were to stay. It was obvious that a few others who were staying there were going to be honoured as we spotted the large hatboxes amongst the luggage. The hotel had a marvellous young doorman in a red coat and top hat, who looked after us rather well.

The following morning we walked to the Palace, passing the friendly policemen who seemed to be everywhere and joined the queue at the gate before 10 o'clock. Then we could see John in the line of cars waiting to come in – these cars were being searched thoroughly and some were taken apart – security was quite an issue and the policemen perhaps not quite so 'friendly' after all.

When we went into the Palace, up the long staircase with its red carpet we lost ourselves in the experience of it all, the soldiers standing like statues, the massive masterpieces on the walls and the hats! We, the recipients were shown to the cloakrooms to leave our coats and then directed to the Picture Gallery where we were told the procedures for the day. I just wanted to look at all the wonderful paintings on every wall – what a waiting room!

Then at 11.00 am it all began and we watched on large television screens the arrival of HRH Prince Charles and his staff. Two Ghurkas accompanied them which was a tradition established by Queen Victoria in 1876. I was grateful that my surname began with a B, as this meant that I was near the beginning of the queue. After we had received our medals we went to the back of the Palace Ballroom to watch the rest of the ceremony. Prince Charles was very easy to talk to as he congratulated me, and then he said he was interested in my work with honeybees in the county of Devon.

Our conversation was about keeping bees and he told me that he had an interesting bee house at Highgrove; "Very ornate and it would amuse you – you must come to visit". I was wearing my Mothers' Union badge (because the Queen is our patron) and also the Devon Air Ambulance silver pin – but no bee badge, so how did the Prince remember to talk about bees?

At the end of the investiture of 104 people, the National Anthem was played again and then the Royal Party walked down through the ballroom. The orchestra of the Coldstream Guards continued to play as we left the ballroom and out to have the official photographs taken at the bottom of the steps. I suppose it was the most exciting day that we had all experienced and after dinner at the hotel we took a taxi to Drury Lane Theatre to see *My Fair Lady*. John has been involved with many musicals during his theatre work such as *South Pacific* and *The Sound of Music* but he had never seen *My Fair Lady*. Norman and I had seen the original production in the 1950s during our courting days with Julie Andrews, Rex Harrison and Stanley Holloway. This performance was just as memorable and it made a perfect ending to an extraordinary day. We returned to our hotel by taxi through the London lights and recognised Marble Arch and all the familiar places and landmarks of London. The joy of this time is still with us when we look at the photographs or the video.

Prince Charles was extremely easy to talk to and our conversation was mostly about honey bees.

My family on the steps of Buckingham Palace.

A VISIT TO HIGHGROVE

About four months later the telephone rang just as we were serving cream teas to visitors to our garden. Usually I would not have answered as we were so busy but I picked up the 'phone and a voice said: "This is Highgrove", then she went on to say: "I am the Prince of Wales' Private Secretary and he apologises that you may think that he had forgotten that he had invited you to Highgrove". Then she explained that a small group of people that His Royal Highness had met this year were being invited on August 7th – so could we come? Well, I did not even bother to look in the diary and just said "yes, please". We looked forward to our visit, which was to start at 11.00 am with great anticipation.

The Prince of Wales purchased Highgrove, near Tetbury in Gloucestershire in 1980. The grounds then consisted of a path around the house, a lawn, and old kitchen garden and a few bushes. It had a very graceful 200 year old Cedar of Lebanon tree with which he fell in love. Now, over twenty years on, the garden and its grounds have been transformed by the Prince of Wales and it reflects his gardening interests and his belief in organic principles.

When we visited we were welcomed in the Orchard Room by the lady who would be our guide. Of course we were asked to make sure we had no cameras, mobile phones or secateurs! I just remember the feeling of peace and tranquillity there and recognising the very familiar square house we have all seen on television or in photographs. The garden is not grand but is rather like a large family garden that has been beautifully planned and laid out. We met several young people during our time there who were enjoying the experience of working in the garden under the Princes Trust scheme.

The garden offers glimpses of the surrounding country and near the drive at the front of the house through to the church at Tetbury. We enjoyed the terrace garden with the fountain and exploring the thyme walk along the pathway to the dovecote. The sundial garden near the south side of the house was full of summer flowers with a black and white colour theme enclosed in box hedge borders. In contrast, the woodland garden with its new 'stumpery' – a great pile of old roots and stumps encourages the lush growth of ferns and euphorbias, hostas and hellebores and then we walked on to the Arboretum.

I suppose for us visiting the cottage garden, with so many familiar plants and then on to the vegetable garden were the parts of Highgrove we enjoyed most. In the walled garden grow vegetables, herbs, flowers, and fruit within the sixteen plots that are edged with low box hedges – it was also encouraging to see some weeds! It is not a show garden but a beloved area planned and enjoyed by the Prince, and everyone who works there or visits during the year. It is run entirely using organic growing methods, aiming to garden in harmony with nature. All the garden waste is used to produce compost and leaf mould to feed nutrients back into the soil. Everything looked healthy and productive.

During our visit, I was taken by one of the gardeners around to the orchard where the bee house, and several beehives stand. Certainly the bee house was very ornate with colourful designs painted above the flight board entrances. It was obvious that black bees occupied these hives and there were large numbers of them at the entrances. Very few of us keep black bees in Devon as they can be difficult to manage due to their aggressive tendencies. Certainly I did not venture too close (without my bee suit) but it was marvellous to be given the opportunity to see them as I remembered my easy conversation about bees with HRH in February. I walked back on my own to meet the group walking past the special henhouse and the Prince's Aberdeen Angus cattle. Then we enjoyed Duchy Originals shortbread biscuits with large pots of tea and coffee served in the Orchard Room.

I had asked if I could take some of our Woodland honey for the Prince of Wales and I received a letter from Mrs Gray, his secretary: 'The Prince of Wales has asked me to write to thank you for your extremely generous gift of honey and candles. His Royal Highness was delighted to receive the gifts and pleased to learn that you had been able to visit the garden here at Highgrove. The Prince of Wales has asked me to send you his best wishes'.

What a day – what an experience, and how lucky we had been.

Highgrove House.

40

DEATH BY GARDENING

In 2002, we had a phone call from the BBC. They said that they were planning a series about the dangers of DIY and accidents in the garden, and would I agree to take part because of my serious injuries falling through our greenhouse. I agreed but asked if the Devon Air Ambulance could be part of it, as I had been rescued by them.

So on a rather wet cold day in February 2003 a film crew arrived here and the day was spent re-enacting my journey through the garden to the greenhouse and then, covered in BBC blood, running back to the house calling for help. In between, repeating it all time and time again, I was covered in a coat and blankets to keep warm! Norman spent a long time with the film crew in the bathroom (because he was getting up and running a bath when I actually had my accident).

The following week we travelled to a house and garden near Bristol, which was set up as an accident-scene set – we needed to arrive by 8.30 am to start filming again. A greenhouse had been erected that was identical to ours with a special glass wall through which the stunt actress would fall. This was also a wet, cold day and this time I had to set up my visit inside the greenhouse, hand over to Denise the stunt lady who would actually fall through the glass, and then covered in 'blood' again I ran out of the door. We wore identical blue shirts and navy trousers, but my shirt was the bloody one! It was quite easy for me to re-enact the accident until I heard the sound of glass breaking – then the director said "again", and the glass wall was replaced for a repeat. That sound really made me feel queasy with the memories of the accident and my left arm ached in sympathy. However, it was a fascinating day and an interesting experience.

We had to wait for a few weeks for the third day of filming because the presenter Tommy Walsh was away filming *Ground Force* programmes in America. Tommy was to be the link person throughout the one-hour programme of gardening accidents. Tommy and the crew arrived here at Orleycombe at 8.30 in the morning and the first thing he said was "I would love a cup of tea, please".

This was another fascinating day with Tommy acting out link shots in our garden and then at 12 o'clock the Air Ambulance flew in to land in our valley. Rob Mackie was the pilot and he was an old pro, having taken part in filming for *Casualty* and other programmes. A sequence was set up with Tommy flying in and they had to refer to our cream teas and the fruit cakes I always take to the airport.

A few local friends had come to serve a ploughman's lunch to the helicopter crew, the BBC and some of the Air Ambulance staff but we had kept quiet about the proposal to land the helicopter because the BBC did not want hoards of people watching. With Tommy and the film crew here it was quite a jolly occasion in between the serious filming sequences.

The programme was finally called *Death by Gardening* and was screened during the summer. The aim was to warn people how easy it is to hurt yourself in the garden, with tools and machinery but we were very pleased that it offered a high profile of the Devon Air Ambulance service. We both enjoyed working with Tommy and the wonderful television crew – they were all good fun to be with.

The Devon Air Ambulance landed in our valley with Tommy, paramedics Dominic and Paul and pilot Rob.

Tommy Walsh.

Planning the next shot.

Eugene, main camera and the film crew at Bristol.

There was a very large BBC crew with cameras, lighting, producer and assistants and an extra producer and fast camera for Denise, who did the fall through the glass. She was quite pleased because this was one stunt she had never done before. She wore a wig the same colour as my hair.

43

THE QUIET GARDEN TRUST

To see a World in a grain of sand
And Heaven in a wild flower,
Hold infinity in the palm of your hand
And Eternity in an hour.

William Blake.

In a garden we are in touch with a special kind of wonder – the colours, the smells, the changes during the seasons and it is always there. We have had a share in creating and working in the garden so it is very special to us. Norman and I love to share our cottage and garden with friends and visitors and it also gives us an extra sense of purpose during the winter months as we plan what seeds and plants to grow. We have been open for charity funds for many years and visitors have commented on how peaceful it is; "You should open as a Quiet Garden" they have often suggested.

So I found out about the Quiet Garden movement, which offers a ministry of hospitality and prayer. 'Come with me by yourselves to a quiet place and get some rest' from Mark: Chapter 6, verse 31. This movement encourages the provision of local venues where there is an opportunity to set aside time to rest and pray. This seems ever more necessary in recent years as life gets more stressful and busy and the traffic on all our roads and lanes in Devon has become increasingly chaotic.

Quiet Gardens and Quiet Spaces come in all shapes and sizes – each one is unique and its owners are encouraged to make provision for local needs. Some open and close the sessions with led meditation or prayer; others offer reflective teaching on different aspects of Christian spirituality and others may just present a place of peace and quiet. In 2004 we affiliated our garden to the Quiet Garden Trust and opened several days during the summer months.

The first garden opened in 1992 at Stoke Poges in Buckinghamshire, because of the vision of Philip Roderick, who is an Anglican priest. One day while enjoying the peace of his own garden it occurred to him that what was needed for a simple ministry of hospitality and prayer was a house and garden – there was no need for expensive premises. Since then the ministry has grown steadily across Britain but after a visit by Philip to the United States of America and Canada a number of gardens have opened there. Many are opening in inner city areas in this country as well. 'Growth is appropriate in anything to do with gardens! The growth of the Quiet Garden movement from one to over two hundred and forty in ten years and across five continents, is a huge achievement in which many hands have been actively involved' writes Esther de Waal, a patron.

'Paradise' is the Greek word for a garden and in the spring when the bank of intense blue of the bluebells and the gold cowslips in the orchard are flowering between the apple blossom, it feels like paradise to us. We love the smell of 'Leaping Salmon' and 'Pensioner' roses, honeysuckles and later, the great profusion of colour in the herbaceous border. The sound of the waterfall and fountain in the pond and the flash of iridescence from the wings of the caddis flies and dragonflies – we feel very blessed when we experience these.

My Garden

A garden is a lovesome thing, God wot!
Rose plot, fringed pool, ferned grot –
The veriest school of peace; and yet the fool
Contends that God is not –
Not God! In gardens! When the eve is cool?
Nay but I have a sign;
'Tis very sure God walks in mine.

by Thomas Edward Brown

Bumble bee on Apple blossom.

45

The herbaceous flower bed in late summer.

OUTREACH TO PRISON

We met Martin, the chaplain at a local prison, at a wedding when our friends Emily and Tim were married by Martin. I sent him a copy of *A New Journey* and when he had read it he telephoned to ask me if I would go to play the piano in the prison chapel. He had realised that I had begun to play the church organ and piano again after my accident – "But I cannot play very well yet" I told him. "That's good, my men don't like anything that is perfect" Martin retorted, so that is how it began.

The first Sunday that I went to the prison I decided not to wear anything too bright or jazzy, so I wore a blue and white striped shirt with a blue skirt, and of course the Mothers' Union badge. To my surprise as the men arrived from their cells they were wearing blue and white shirts and blue trousers! I did hope that I would be let out again after the service!

For the last five years I have visited regularly on a Sunday to worship in the chapel and Caroline (Emily's mother) and I have been involved in offering 'Parenting' courses to the men. These courses needed to be adjusted from the usual parenting syllabus, which would involve trying different ways of communicating with your children. In some cases, the men have lost touch with their youngsters but there is still a great need to care. They may feel extremely guilty and sometimes their children do not even know where they are – as one said "My son thinks I am working abroad".

I know as a mother and a teacher, how important our own experiences of our parents guiding and leading us. Some of the men in prison have received little or no parenting themselves and in fact some have been in care throughout their growing up. They have no foundations on which to base their own parenting skills. The courses seemed to be well accepted and we hope that we may have given the men some new insights into how they can communicate with their families, especially when they are released from prison.

Caroline and I have always shared with pride the fact that we belong to the Mothers' Union, which is a worldwide organisation whose purpose is to be concerned with all aspects of Christian family life. It was founded in 1876 by Mary Sumner, the wife of an Anglican vicar. When their first child was born she was overwhelmed by the awesome responsibility of being a parent, so she started support groups for young families. One of the aims is to help those whose family life has met with adversity.

Now there are over three million members in over seventy countries and we support family life both at home and overseas. We work in wide areas such as literacy and HIV/Aids abroad, and prisons and parenting courses in the United Kingdom. Unfortunately the Mothers' Union has an old-fashioned image as the 'tea makers' but the breadth of work going on is amazing. There are over seventy prisons being visited by members in this country alone, so our work in Devon is very important.

At Christmas, there are several carol concerts held in the prisons and we provide Mothers' Union serviettes with the mince pies. One young man who received one last year told me he had kept the serviette with our logo on it in his cell for the rest of the year.

Lord, you offer freedom to all people.
We pray for all those who are in prison.
Support with your love, prisoners, their families and friends, prison staff
and all who care.
Amen.

STUMPWORK MIRROR

When I retired I had planned to spend many hours each week using the wood turning lathe in our linhay. John had bought one and set it up on a bench and over the years I had a good collection of different woods to use. I had first learned to turn wood on a holiday course at the Old School House, in Middleham in Yorkshire. Elizabeth was working in the Yorkshire Dales and my friends Margaret and Shirley went to stay there too – they did a weaving and embroidery course while I was covered in wood shavings in the lathe workshop! I learned some more advanced techniques at Dartington after that but I was looking forward to having plenty of time to do a lot of woodturning in my retirement. The accident to my arm was severe so I knew that it could never manage the force of a lathe, so the woodturning machinery had to go.

Apparently as a small child I enjoyed making things, often tiny animals from acorns and beechnuts, and I loved to draw and paint. My grandmother taught me how to knit and use the old Singer sewing machine. I remember her showing me how to make jams and marmalade too, so there was no lack of incentive for me to find creative things to do.

In our small parish of Woodland we had a group of people keen to make kneelers for the church. We designed our own patterns and some of the later ones were pictures of the farms and cottages that we live in. Finally we made the long altar kneelers, using a fine pattern of lilies designed by Shirley. The background colour was a dark shade of burgundy wool, which matched the carpet in the church. Someone suggested that we could make the map of Woodland using canvas squares and so the Woodland tapestry was planned. Twenty-seven local people took part and it became a real community effort.

We used the 1837 Parish Map for the design, with a border to include the names of properties and fields together with pictures of Woodland's flora and fauna. It is woven together with a scrolling peach-coloured ribbon. The wall hanging now measures eight feet by ten feet and it hangs on the main wall of the Woodland Parish Room. We had a big gathering of parishioners with the flags hung out across the village square to celebrate its completion. I was involved with the tapestry project during the early years following my accident – the stitching work certainly made my hand and arm hurt, but I am sure that it also helped to strengthen them.

So how do you follow that? I belong to the West Country Embroiderers, which was started many years ago to encourage ladies to meet together and to develop their sewing skills. There are many groups across Cornwall, Devon and Dorset, and every two years we set up an exhibition of our work within one of these counties. Last year when it was Devon's turn we used Rosemoor Royal Horticultural Society Gardens and the theme, of course, was the natural world. It was a perfect setting looking through the windows of the exhibition room to the colourful garden beyond.

I have enjoyed many day schools during these years where I learnt the techniques of hardanger, blackwork, goldwork and stumpwork to name just a few. Often I use the completed piece of work to make into a book cover or the lid of a box. Beadwork is very addictive too, and the variety of colours and shapes of beads look just like a collection of sweeties! Amulet purses, needle-cases and tiny bags are so satisfying to make and I also love to incorporate beads into my embroidery.

One square of the Woodland Tapestry.

Then I went to a day school workshop to learn the beginnings of stumpwork – I think I achieved one green leaf that day but I was 'hooked'! This technique of three-dimensional embroidery was popular during the seventeenth century and it was called stumpwork, because the work was raised with 'stumps' of wood or pads of wool. It was usually worked on fine linen canvas or an ivory-coloured silk. The finished samples of work would be used in pictures, caskets or mirror frames.

We had seen some wonderful examples of stumpwork when we visited the Burrell Collection in Glasgow, with Elizabeth and Jeremy. After that I began to research the subject and hunted down examples of such work. Several stumpwork pictures are at Trerice, in north Cornwall and then I saw the mirror in the White Bedroom at Cotehele. This was completed in 1668 by Margaret Hall. I knew that I wanted to make one for the twenty first century and that it should be inspired by our Orleycombe garden. Drawings and photographs would guide the designs. This became my winter project and I would even awaken in the middle of the night thinking about it; "I realise I haven't included a ladybird", or; "shall I embroider clematis or the passion flower?"

'More than anything, I must have flowers, always, always'.

Claude Monet.

And so it was on the four sections of stumpwork or raised embroidery – wild strawberries, violets and primroses, the periwinkle that shines blue along the hedges, roses and clematis. Then, acorns and the small black grapes that grow along the fence near the orchard. A bumblebee, honeybee, ladybird, dragonfly and a hedgehog hiding under the dandelion leaves. It also has the tiny blue butterfly that we now see so often on the wild flowers in the orchard – and the shiny black spider on her web.

Then I met Tom Parker, a wood turner and carpenter, who made me a frame for it so beautifully from Devonshire oak wood. Neither of us really knew how it would work, but the four pieces of embroidery slipped into place perfectly and the mirror now hangs near our front door for visitors to use and enjoy. Now I plan to make another stumpwork mirror for Elizabeth, this time using seashore designs.

Stumpwork mirror.

51

THE LAUNCH OF THE NEW AIR AMBULANCE

So the 'state of the art' EC135 has arrived to serve the people of Devon after several years of planning and the raising of funds for it. This means running costs will increase from £1.5 million to £1.8 million a year, with additional operational costs. The Devon Air Ambulance lottery has been run by the Trust staff since September 2001 with enormous success, and it goes from strength to strength to support the new helicopter.

There are many advantages to the EC135, which will mean that patients will get to hospital more quickly and there is more room inside for the paramedics to manoeuvre and look after you. There is an extra passenger seat so that if a child is airlifted then a parent can go along too. It also has additional space to carry an incubator. It is a wonderful, technologically advanced aircraft that will serve the people of Devon very well for decades to come.

Powderham Castle was the venue chosen to launch the new helicopter. It

The EC135 helicopter lands at Powderham.

was a perfect sunny day, and we had the backdrop of the castle, the gardens and the vast grounds stretching to the banks of the river Exe. We have often seen this view from the train as it passes and everyone looks out for the fallow deer grazing everywhere.

Hundreds of people were invited to the castle to arrive at mid-day and it was a chance to thank staff, crew, volunteers and fund-raisers. Everyone had a marvellous time – there was music in the background and the smell of sausages cooking. Exactly at 12.30 pm we all looked up into the sky when we heard the familiar sound – the new helicopter flew slowly above us, escorted by the old Bolkow and a police helicopter. It could be compared to the Red Arrows in formation, but in slow motion! Everyone cheered and clapped as the three aircraft landed.

Steve Ford was the pilot of the new helicopter and a pilot from Wales flew the Bolkow, from where it was to go into service. Somehow it was good to see the familiar shape that has meant so much to those of us who have been rescued. Of course, after the VIP's, the press and television crews, had viewed the aircraft all the visitors could look as well – what excitement there was! Piers and I were pleased to see Chay Farzaneh, who was one of the very first Junior Crew Club members. He has recently finished his college course and has been offered a post at Ambulance Control – how amazing it will be if he becomes a flying paramedic one day!

The celebration cakes were cut and I am sure that many good thoughts and wishes were made for the future year of the service.

With Piers, Rob and Chay at Powderham.

53

AND SO TO THE FUTURE

What might have been and what has been
Point to one end, which is always present.
Footfalls echo in the memory
Down the passage we did not take,
Towards the door we never opened.

T. S. Eliot

Memory cannot be separated from the passage of time and for each one of us our memories will vary because of our experiences of life. Certainly the past ten years have offered varied, often happy but sometimes sad experiences for our family. We have been privileged to meet many different people and to share our home and garden with some of them.

Memories are precious and somehow the good ones seem to become foremost. I have never felt the need to ask "Why me?" when things have been disappointing – I just feel that for each one of us life is a journey and we have to cope as best we can. Some of the unhappy times can give you an empathy for others in trouble and our Christian faith gives us a strength to try to help those in need.

Mother Teresa wrote: 'Be happy in the moment, that's enough. Each moment is all we need, not more. Be happy now and if you show through your actions that you love others, including those who are poorer than you, you'll give them happiness too. It doesn't take much – it can be just giving a smile. The world would be a much better place if everyone smiled more. So smile, be cheerful, be joyous that God loves you'.

The healing of my arm took a very long time and in fact continues even ten years later. I think we all expect to be better after any illness or accident very quickly but the body and spirit need time to rest and to be restored. In a way I was lucky that my friends expected me to continue all the activities I took part in and our Orleycombe group came here regularly to embroider, to exchange books and magazines and to offer each other new ideas. At first I had to sew with one hand using a large frame on a stand but it is amazing how quickly we adapt to a different technique.

I enjoyed weaving on a frame, with Pat Johns, a well known tapestry weaver, guiding us all and we worked hard towards having an exhibition of our work. One of my first pieces was a weaving of our old cottage, set against the fields and sloping woods as a background. Then I did one in gold hexagons with several honeybees and this was sold at the first exhibition, much to my surprise.

Since then I have done one of BUZZ to practise weaving lettering and everyone thought that this was the buzz of my honeybees, but I suspect it is the sound we all make when we are working! Pat dyes her own wools which we use and it is a joy to handle and choose such a variety of colours and textures.

Several friends have joined the weaving group and now we have regular workshop days at Pat's home in Exeter. We can enjoy and marvel at her work on the walls and it inspires us to try to improve. Elizabeth has spent a week with Pat weaving on a frame and she followed this with a course to learn to make felt. Our daughter Elizabeth is an inspiration to us because with short arms and without thumbs she often uses her feet. Recently I had my first attempt to make felt and perhaps using my feet would have given a better result. Over the ten years I have had to accept that there are some daily tasks and activities that are now difficult. I have learnt it can be very satisfying to find other ways and alternative hobbies instead.

In *A New Journey* I wrote a chapter about coping with pain and during the past ten years I have become used to having some pain in my left arm and hand. In a way, I felt grateful for it because it demonstrated that the damaged parts were working again. In the last few years the pain has been increasing and I have had new pains in my feet and legs, especially when I am tired or have been standing for too long. I was encouraged to visit the Arcturus Clinic in Totnes to receive acupuncture, which is a Chinese method of treating the body and its disorders. Acupuncture aims to strengthen our vitality and to restore balance to our whole bodily constitution, rather than looking for a specific symptom and treating that, usually with a drug that can cause side effects and may weaken the body and its energy. I am astonished at the way that acupuncture has relieved my pain over the past few months of treatment and I feel more relaxed than I have done for many years.

We are very lucky that we live in a beautiful part of our country. There is so much beauty around us but we need to take the time to notice it. It can be so joyful to watch the birds feeding on our bird tables, especially when seven or eight long-tailed tits come together to feed or we spot the bright colours of the greater spotted woodpecker – they are extremely shy birds. To see the delicacy of the tiny blue butterflies flitting from wild flowers to feed – their perfect form, colour and the markings around their wings. The shape of trees, flowers, the smell of grass and the sound of running water – the joy of life's small moments. My journey ten years on has been good – I will not be concerned for the future.

Then shall I know...
　　Not till the loom is silent
And the shuttles cease to fly,
　　Shall God unroll the canvas
And explain the reason why
　　The dark threads are as needful
In the weaver's skilful hand
　　As the threads of gold and silver
In the pattern He has planned.